INSIDE THE NFL

SAN FRANCISCO 49ERS

by Ted Coleman

Abdo & Daughters
MIDDLE GRADE NONFICTION

An imprint of Abdo Publishing
abdobooks.com

ABDOBOOKS.COM

Published by Abdo Publishing, a division of ABDO, PO Box 398166, Minneapolis, Minnesota 55439.

Printed in China.
052025
092025

Cover Photos: Ezra Shaw/Getty Images Sport/Getty Images (Christian McCaffrey); Jed Jacobsohn/Allsport/Getty Images Sport/Getty Images (Jerry Rice)
Interior Photos: Cooper Neill/Getty Images Sport/Getty Images, 4–5, 6, 11, 61 (bottom right); Thearon W. Henderson/Getty Images Sport/Getty Images, 7, 8; Lachlan Cunningham/Getty Images Sport/Getty Images, 9; Michael Zagaris/San Francisco 49ers/Getty Images Sport/Getty Images, 10, 53, 59; Abdo Publishing, 12–13, 58; NFL Photos/AP Images, 14–15, 60 (bottom left); Hy Peskin Archive/Archive Photos/Getty Images, 16; Ray Howard/AP Images, 17; Sporting News Archive/Getty Images, 19; Hulton Archive/Getty Images, 20; Focus on Sport/Getty Images, 21, 22, 46; Focus on Sport/Getty Images Sport/Getty Images, 23, 24, 33, 36, 40, 44, 61 (bottom left); Tony Tomsic/AP Images, 25, 31, 60 (bottom right); Richard J. Doyle/Archive Photos/Getty Images, 26–27; David Madison/Getty Images Sport/Getty Images, 28, 48–49, 60 (top); Rob Brown/Getty Images Sport/Getty Images, 29, 63; Peter Read Miller/AP Images, 30, 35; Bettmann/Getty Images, 34, 61 (top left); John Biever/Sports Illustrated/Getty Images, 37; Otto Greule Jr./Getty Images Sport/Getty Images, 38–39; Bill Haber/AP Images, 41; Al Golub/AP Images, 42; Paul Spinelli/AP Images, 43; John G. Mabanglo/AFP/Getty Images, 45; Greg Trott/AP Images, 47, 50; Ezra Shaw/Getty Images Sport/Getty Images, 52; Jamie Squire/Getty Images Sport/Getty Images, 54, 57, 61 (top right); Marcio Jose Sanchez/AP Images, 55

Editor: Haley Williams
Series Designer: Laura Graphenteen
Production Designer: Ryan Gale

Library of Congress Control Number: 2024948473

Publisher's Cataloging-in-Publication Data

Names: Coleman, Ted, author.
Title: San Francisco 49ers / by Ted Coleman
Description: Minneapolis, Minnesota: Abdo Publishing, 2026 | Series: Inside the NFL | Includes online resources and index.
Identifiers: ISBN 9781098296896 (lib. bdg.) | ISBN 9798384919414 (ebook)
Subjects: LCSH: San Francisco 49ers (Football team)--Juvenile literature. | National Football League--Juvenile literature. | Football teams--Juvenile literature. | American football--Juvenile literature.
Classification: DDC 796.33264--dc23

CONTENTS

The San Francisco 49ers run onto the field at Levi's Stadium before the NFC Championship Game against the Detroit Lions in January 2024.

CHAPTER 1

EIGHT MINUTES OF MAGIC

SOMETIMES, A NATIONAL FOOTBALL LEAGUE (NFL) TEAM NEEDS A little bit of luck or magic. On January 28, 2024, the San Francisco 49ers were looking for either. Facing the Detroit Lions, the 49ers were trailing 24–7 heading into halftime of the National Football Conference (NFC) Championship Game. San Francisco was hoping to turn things around in the second half.

Nothing had gone right for the 49ers in the first half against the Lions. Playing at home at Levi's Stadium in Santa Clara, California, the 49ers were favored to win. But their normally tough defense gave up a series of big plays, and their offense stalled. Brock Purdy, who was usually sound at quarterback, threw an ugly interception. The Lions capitalized on every opportunity and took a big lead by halftime.

Quarterback Brock Purdy rushed for 48 yards and threw for 267 yards and a touchdown in the playoff game against the Lions.

OVER THE HUMP

After a slow start to the 2023 season, the 49ers appeared on their way to their third loss in the NFC title game in three seasons. Two years earlier, the team had blown a 10-point fourth-quarter lead against the Los Angeles Rams and lost 20–17. Then Purdy and backup Josh Johnson suffered injuries during the next season's conference championship. Although Purdy eventually returned to the game with a hurt elbow, the Philadelphia Eagles rocked the 49ers 31–7.

In order for the 49ers to avoid a third straight loss, they needed a total team effort. The first sign of life from them came in the third quarter. Purdy finally settled in and led a field-goal drive to pull the 49ers back within 14 points. But the Lions got the ball back and were looking to extend their lead.

TAKING ADVANTAGE

The Lions had the ball at the San Francisco 30 with just under eight minutes to go in the third. On third-and-four, Detroit quarterback Jared Goff handed the ball to star receiver Amon-Ra St. Brown. Standout San Francisco linebacker Fred Warner met St. Brown head-on and held him to a 2-yard gain. On the next play, Detroit coach Dan Campbell decided to gamble and go for the first down rather than kick a field goal. Goff fired a pass over the middle for receiver Josh Reynolds, who dropped the ball.

Reynolds's drop was the luck San Francisco needed.

Linebacker Fred Warner led the 49ers with 13 tackles in the NFC title game.

Receiver Brandon Aiyuk (11) catches a touchdown in the third quarter of the NFC title game.

With momentum on their side, the 49ers got the ball back. After a completion brought the ball to the San Francisco 45-yard line, the 49ers decided to go for a big play. Purdy threw a deep pass down the middle of the field to receiver Brandon Aiyuk. However, Purdy threw the ball too hard. Detroit cornerback Kindle Vildor angled for the interception. Instead, the ball ricocheted off Vildor's face mask. As the defender fell down, the ball bounced back toward Aiyuk, who made a diving catch at the 4-yard line.

Three plays later, Purdy and Aiyuk connected on a 6-yard touchdown pass to cut Detroit's lead to 24–17. Aiyuk later admitted that luck was on his side on the big play. "Before the game, a ladybug landed on my shoe," he said. "Y'all know what that means. So that's all that I can say. . . . Just great luck."

FINISHING THE JOB

When the Lions got the ball back, the home crowd was feeling the magic. On Detroit's first play, Goff handed off to rookie running back Jahmyr Gibbs. San Francisco safety Tashaun Gipson smacked Gibbs and knocked the ball loose. The stadium then erupted as 49ers defensive lineman Arik Armstead recovered at Detroit's 24-yard line.

Purdy was a steady passer, but he was not known as a great scrambler. Yet, with his receivers covered on first down, he took off up the middle. The second-year quarterback then broke toward the left sideline and raced 21 yards to the Lions' 4-yard line. Then running back Christian McCaffrey scored from 1-yard out. Kicker Jake Moody's extra point tied the game 24–24.

In a span of eight minutes, the 49ers had erased a 17-point deficit. And they kept rolling into the fourth quarter. Another field goal by Moody and a 3-yard touchdown run from Elijah Mitchell put San Francisco up 34–24. By the time the Lions scored again with under a minute left, it was too late.

MR. IRRELEVANT

Quarterback Brock Purdy was the last player chosen in the 2022 NFL Draft. That pick is often referred to as "Mr. Irrelevant." This is because historically, players chosen in that spot have struggled to make NFL teams. However, during the 2023 season, Purdy became the first Mr. Irrelevant to play in the Super Bowl and be selected for the Pro Bowl.

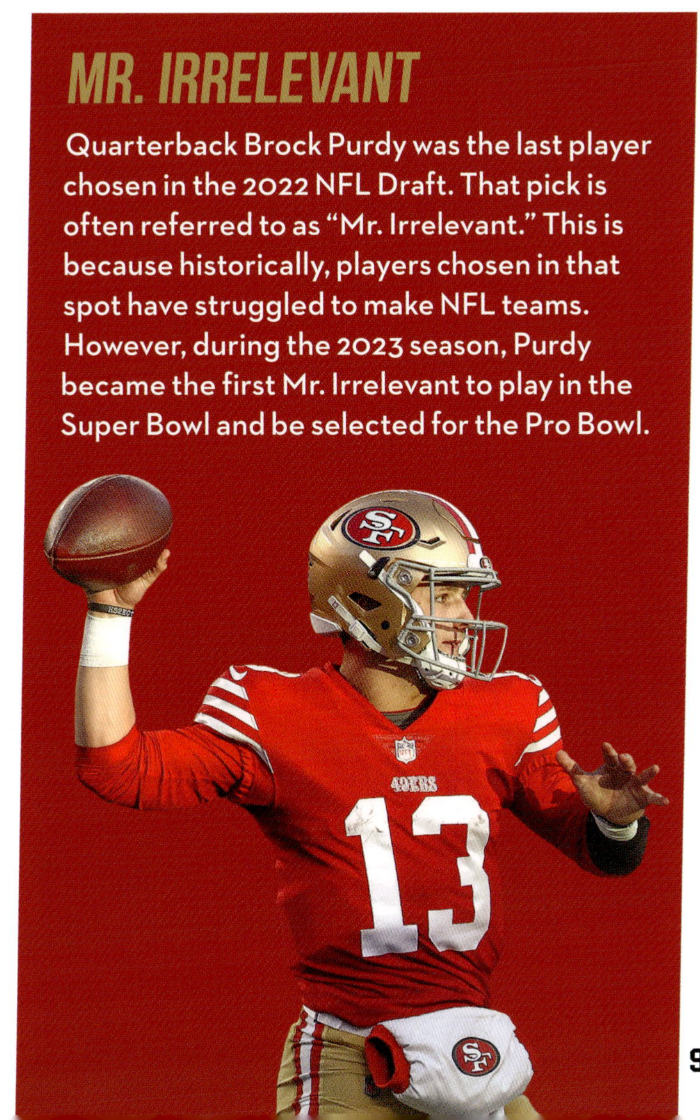

Running back Christian McCaffrey (23) rushed for 90 yards and two touchdowns against the Lions.

Offensive lineman Trent Williams celebrates after the 49ers' victory over Detroit in the NFC Championship Game.

The crowd knew the 49ers were on their way to Super Bowl LVIII. And the win against the Lions was all thanks to a magical sequence of events that turned the game upside down. "Obviously, nobody wins without a little luck," said 49ers offensive lineman Trent Williams after the game. "Tonight was just our time to get it."

"OBVIOUSLY, NOBODY WINS WITHOUT A LITTLE LUCK. TONIGHT WAS JUST OUR TIME TO GET IT."

—TRENT WILLIAMS

NFL TEAMS MAP

NFC EAST

-  DALLAS COWBOYS
-  NEW YORK GIANTS
-  PHILADELPHIA EAGLES
-  WASHINGTON COMMANDERS

NFC WEST

-  ARIZONA CARDINALS
-  LOS ANGELES RAMS
-  SAN FRANCISCO 49ERS
-  SEATTLE SEAHAWKS

NFC NORTH

-  CHICAGO BEARS
-  DETROIT LIONS
-  GREEN BAY PACKERS
-  MINNESOTA VIKINGS

NFC SOUTH

-  ATLANTA FALCONS
-  CAROLINA PANTHERS
-  NEW ORLEANS SAINTS
- TAMPA BAY BUCCANEERS

AFC

AFC EAST

- BUFFALO BILLS
- MIAMI DOLPHINS
- NEW ENGLAND PATRIOTS
- NEW YORK JETS

AFC WEST

- DENVER BRONCOS
- KANSAS CITY CHIEFS
- LAS VEGAS RAIDERS
- LOS ANGELES CHARGERS

AFC NORTH

- BALTIMORE RAVENS
- CINCINNATI BENGALS
- CLEVELAND BROWNS
- PITTSBURGH STEELERS

AFC SOUTH

-  HOUSTON TEXANS
-  INDIANAPOLIS COLTS
-  JACKSONVILLE JAGUARS
- TENNESSEE TITANS

Quarterback Frankie Albert threw 14 touchdown passes during the 49ers' first season in 1946.

CHAPTER 2

CALIFORNIA'S ORIGINAL TEAM

BACK IN 1942, PROFESSIONAL FOOTBALL IN CALIFORNIA WAS JUST AN idea. One of the people who wanted to make that idea a reality was San Francisco businessman Tony Morabito. Professional football in those days was mostly popular in the Midwest and on the East Coast. But Morabito believed the sport could succeed in Northern California.

Morabito first requested for the NFL to add a franchise in San Francisco in 1942, but his bid was quickly rejected. He tried again in 1944 but got the same answer. The NFL's westernmost team was in Chicago, and the league did not see the need to expand any farther.

Morabito did not give up on his dream of West Coast football, though. Instead of the NFL, he started a team in the newly formed league called the All-America Football Conference (AAFC).

The AAFC was set to begin play in 1946.

THE AAFC YEARS

In the mid-1950s, the 49ers sported red helmets as a part of their uniforms.

Before the team could take the field, it needed a name. One of the team owners, Allen E. Sorrell, suggested "49ers." The 1849 gold rush was an important event in Northern California, as it dramatically increased the wealth and population in the area. Those who traveled to California that year hoping to find gold and strike it rich were known as 49ers. Despite the team's ties to the gold rush, the 49ers played their first few seasons in red jerseys and either silver or white pants. The team didn't start wearing its familiar red and gold colors until the 1960s.

No matter their colors, the 49ers struggled to strike gold in the AAFC. The league lasted four seasons. San Francisco had a winning record in each of them with help from players such as quarterback

Frankie Albert and fullback Joe Perry. But the team was no match for the dominant Cleveland Browns. The 49ers finished second to Cleveland in the league's West division in each of the AAFC's first three years. In 1949, the league went to a single division. After finishing second to the Browns again, San Francisco met Cleveland in the title game. Albert threw a 23-yard touchdown pass to receiver Paul Salata early in the fourth quarter to cut into Cleveland's 14-point lead, but the 49ers lost 21–7.

Fullback Joe Perry, *with the ball*, played 14 seasons with San Francisco.

THE MILLION DOLLAR BACKFIELD

By the time the 49ers played the Browns in the 1949 title game, both teams knew it was the final game for the AAFC. The league was folding, but three of its teams were headed to the NFL. The dominant Browns were an obvious choice. Joining them were the Baltimore Colts and the 49ers.

In the eight years after the NFL had initially rejected Morabito's bid, the league had changed its mind about West Coast football. In 1946, the NFL's Cleveland Rams had moved to Los Angeles. By adding the 49ers, the league now had a western rivalry between those two teams.

The Rams dominated the early meetings. The 49ers went 1–5 against their southern rival in their first three NFL seasons. Morabito knew his team needed improvements, and he was willing to pay for them. Although health problems slowed the owner down, he ignored his doctor's advice to leave football behind. "If I'm going to die, I might as well die at a football game," he once said.

> **"IF I'M GOING TO DIE, I MIGHT AS WELL DIE AT A FOOTBALL GAME."**
>
> **—TONY MORABITO**

In 1952, Morabito added halfback Hugh McElhenny to San Francisco's backfield alongside Perry. The team also had a strong-armed quarterback in Y. A. Tittle. The trio led the 49ers to a 9–3 record in 1953. It wasn't good enough to reach the NFL title game, but the 49ers beat the Rams twice that year.

After the season, Morabito added another strong rusher. While Perry was on his way to becoming the league's all-time leading rusher and McElhenny added speed, John Henry Johnson simply

Halfback Hugh McElhenny was named to the Pro Bowl five times with the 49ers.

Quarterback Y. A. Tittle led the NFL with 17 touchdown passes in 1955.

ran over defenders. All three running backs ended up in the Pro Football Hall of Fame, alongside Tittle. Sportswriters called the group "the Million Dollar Backfield."

CHANGES AT THE TOP

By 1957, Johnson was gone, but the 49ers still had their three other Hall of Famers. Albert had become the head coach the year prior, and San Francisco started off the 1957 season 3–1. In Week 5, the team faced the Chicago Bears at home. At halftime, with the Bears leading 17–7, someone handed Albert a note. It read, "Tony's gone."

While watching the game, Morabito had collapsed and died. After learning of their owner's death, the 49ers rallied to beat the Bears 21–17. They then finished the season with three straight victories to tie the Detroit Lions for the top spot in the NFL's West division. The teams played a one-game playoff to determine a champion. The 49ers opened up a 24–7 halftime lead, but they couldn't hold it. The Lions rallied, and San Francisco lost 31–27.

The 49ers had just four winning seasons in the 1960s.

ENDING A LONG WAIT

As painful as that loss was, the 1957 season was the team's last high point for a while. During the 1960s, the 49ers were prolific on offense behind strong-armed quarterback John Brodie, but the team struggled to contain opponents. Despite playing high-scoring games, the 49ers never finished higher

THE SHOTGUN

Facing a stingy Baltimore Colts defense in 1960, 49ers coach Howard "Red" Hickey tried an offensive experiment. He had quarterback John Brodie line up 7 yards behind the line of scrimmage. That way, Brodie had a head start on dropping back to pass against the Colts' fierce pass rush. Over time, Hickey's formation, which was called "shotgun," caught on. It is still widely used by football teams at all levels today.

Tight end Ted Kwalick hauls in a pass during the 49ers' playoff game against the Minnesota Vikings in December 1970.

than third place in their division during the decade.

In 1968, the team hired defensive-minded head coach Dick Nolan. By 1970, he had turned the defense into a strong unit led by durable linebacker Dave Wilcox. The 35-year-old Brodie had one of his best seasons, throwing for a league-best 2,941 yards and 24 touchdowns en route to the NFL's Most Valuable Player (MVP) Award. The 49ers finished 10–3–1 and won their division, which was now called the NFC West, for the first time in 14 years.

San Francisco's reward was a trip to frigid Minnesota for a divisional-round game against the Vikings. Brodie shook off the cold weather and threw for 201 yards and a touchdown along with rushing for a second score. The 49ers' defense forced four turnovers in an upset 17–14 win. Suddenly, San Francisco was one step away from the Super Bowl. To get there, the 49ers had to go through Nolan's old team, the Dallas Cowboys. But the 49ers' magical season came to a rough end as Brodie threw two pick sixes in the 17–10 loss.

Quarterback John Brodie recorded 31,548 passing yards during his 17 seasons with the 49ers.

ONE LAST RUN

Brodie was not always a fan favorite in San Francisco. The quarterback mixed in moments of brilliance with erratic play. During the 1971 regular season, he threw 24 interceptions. Despite that, San Francisco still won its division and hosted Washington in the divisional round of the playoffs.

In the third quarter, Brodie delivered the game's biggest play, hitting Pro Bowl receiver Gene Washington on a 78-yard touchdown pass to tie the game 10-10. The 49ers went on to win 24-20 to reach another NFC title game. Their opponent was Dallas for the second year in a row. And once again, the Cowboys' sturdy defense was too much for San Francisco to overcome. The 49ers lost 14-3.

Backup quarterback Steve Spurrier started nine games in 1972 while Brodie was injured.

Nolan and Brodie put together one more run in 1972. Although Brodie was out for most of the year due to an ankle injury, the team won five of its last six games of the regular season to once again secure the division title. This time, San Francisco hosted Dallas in the divisional round. Led by three touchdowns from running back Larry Schreiber, the 49ers took a 28-13 lead into the fourth quarter. But their defense was unable to hold off a furious Cowboys rally, and San Francisco lost 30-28.

Once again, the 49ers had reached a high point. Brodie retired after struggling through the 1973 season. San Francisco embarked on a streak of seven losing seasons in eight years. Nolan was fired

Receiver Gene Washington caught 59 touchdown passes for the 49ers between 1969 and 1977.

after the 1975 season, and the next four coaches couldn't turn San Francisco around. The team hit a low point in 1978 by finishing 2–14, the worst record in the history of the franchise. A big change in team philosophy was clearly needed. And San Francisco's next hire was ready to change the game of football forever.

Bill Walsh won 92 games in 10 seasons as the 49ers' head coach.

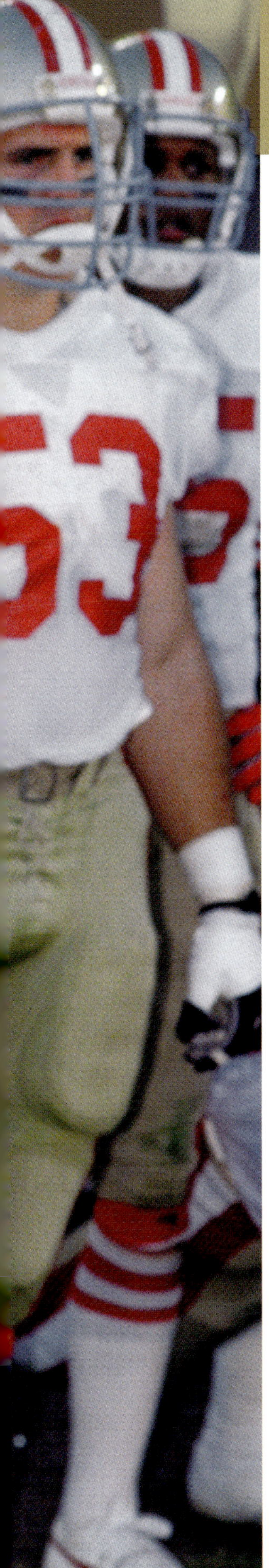

CHAPTER 3

WEST COAST MASTERS

Bill Walsh was one of the most intellectual coaches to ever walk an NFL sideline. When the 49ers hired the longtime assistant and college coach in 1979, some people wondered whether he was tough enough to be an NFL head coach. Oakland Raiders owner Al Davis asked Walsh about that, and Walsh politely reminded Davis that he had been an amateur boxer in his youth.

Walsh was tasked with turning around the struggling 49ers. He wanted to implement his preferred offense, which called for short, quick passes executed with precise timing. Although he had developed the offense while he was an assistant with the Cincinnati Bengals, it became known as "the West Coast offense" after he perfected the system in San Francisco. To run it, Walsh selected quarterback Joe Montana out of Notre Dame in the third round of the 1979 draft. Many scouts questioned Montana's arm strength. But Walsh knew that the young quarterback's intelligence and coolness under pressure were a perfect fit for the new 49ers.

Quarterback Joe Montana was voted to seven Pro Bowls during his time with the 49ers.

Also in 1979, Walsh drafted sure-handed wide receiver Dwight Clark. Neither Clark nor Montana played much that year as the 49ers finished 2–14 again. But in 1980, they were both in the lineup for the game that helped turn the team around. In Week 14, the 49ers trailed the winless New Orleans Saints 35–7 at the end of the first half. In his halftime speech, Walsh admitted he thought the team would lose, but he told his players to just go out and play hard.

Montana responded by rushing for a touchdown and throwing two more scores, the first being a 71-yard strike to Clark in the third quarter. San Francisco rallied to win 38–35 in overtime. At the time, it was the largest comeback in NFL history.

THE CATCH

In 1981, the 49ers broke through with a 13–3 record and the NFC West title. Montana led the league in completion percentage while throwing passes to Clark and star receiver Freddie Solomon. Walsh had bolstered the secondary before the season by drafting defensive players Ronnie Lott, Carlton Williamson, and Eric Wright. All three players eventually made the Pro Bowl, and Lott, one of the most ferocious hitters in league history, eventually reached the Hall of Fame.

After knocking off the New York Giants in the divisional round of the playoffs, the 49ers hosted their old nemesis, the Dallas Cowboys, in the NFC Championship Game. Early in the fourth quarter, the Cowboys went up 27–21 on a 21-yard touchdown pass. But later in the quarter, Montana led the 49ers down the field.

With less than one minute to go, San Francisco had the ball at the Dallas 6-yard line. Montana rolled out

Defensive back Ronnie Lott returned three of his seven interceptions for touchdowns during his rookie season in 1981.

Wide receiver Dwight Clark goes to spike the ball after making "the Catch" in the NFC title game in January 1982.

to his right, where he was chased by three Cowboys defenders. Off his back foot, he heaved a pass to the back of the end zone. It looked to be sailing out of bounds. But then Clark stretched out his 6-foot-4-inch frame and snagged the pass for the winning touchdown. "The Catch," as it was later called, became one of the most famous plays in NFL history, and it brought the 49ers to their first Super Bowl.

THE STAND

San Francisco faced the Cincinnati Bengals in Super Bowl XVI on January 24, 1982. The 49ers dominated the first half, taking a 20–0 lead behind both a rushing and passing touchdown from Montana.

But Cincinnati scored early in the third quarter and was threatening again later in the quarter. The Bengals faced first-and-goal inside the 49ers' 5-yard line.

Cincinnati tried running plays on both first and second down, but the 49ers stopped Bengals fullback Pete Johnson both times. On third down, the Bengals tossed a pass to running back Charles Alexander. San Francisco linebacker Dan Bunz flattened Alexander short of the goal line as he caught the pass. Cincinnati tried to plunge in with Alexander on fourth down, but the 49ers stopped that play as well.

Defensive tackle Archie Reese (78) celebrates on top of a pileup after the 49ers stopped the Cincinnati Bengals from scoring during Super Bowl XVI in January 1982.

The tremendous goal-line stand kept San Francisco ahead for the rest of the game. Although the Bengals scored two late touchdowns to make the game closer, San Francisco won 26–21 to secure its first Super Bowl title. Montana was named the Super Bowl MVP. "Montana will be the great quarterback of the future," said Walsh. "He is one of the coolest competitors of all time, and he has just started."

"MONTANA WILL BE THE GREAT QUARTERBACK OF THE FUTURE. HE IS ONE OF THE COOLEST COMPETITORS OF ALL TIME, AND HE HAS JUST STARTED."

—BILL WALSH

HIGH STEPS

While Walsh's new champions had the look of a dynasty, three years passed before San Francisco made it back to the Super Bowl. In 1984, the 49ers steamrolled their division, finishing 15–1 and waltzing past the Giants and Chicago Bears in the playoffs to reach Super Bowl XIX. One of the team's biggest stars had been dual-threat running back Roger Craig, a former hurdler in high school who used his signature high-knee running style to rush for more than 600 yards. He also caught a team-high 71 passes.

Montana threw a career-best 28 touchdown passes during the 1984 season. However, he was overshadowed by Miami Dolphins quarterback Dan Marino, who set an NFL record by throwing 48 scores. Marino then led the Dolphins to the Super Bowl, and his historic performance dominated the pregame hype. But come game time, Montana and Craig stole the show.

Craig became the first player in Super Bowl history to score three touchdowns as he caught two scores and rushed for another. The 49ers routed Miami 38–16 to win their second Super Bowl title.

Running back Roger Craig hurdles over a Miami Dolphins defender during Super Bowl XIX on January 20, 1985.

Late in the game, San Francisco guard Randy Cross looked into a camera along the sideline and said, "[They] came to see an offense, and the wrong one showed up!"

A NEW WEAPON

The 49ers boasted one of the NFL's best offenses in the early 1980s. But their offense got even better in 1985. With the 16th pick in that year's NFL Draft, the team selected wide receiver Jerry Rice out of Mississippi Valley State. Rice was tall and lean, and he blew past defensive backs with his long, graceful strides. Although Rice struggled early in his rookie season, he went on to have one of the greatest receiving careers in NFL history.

In 1987, Rice had established himself as the league's best pass catcher by hauling in an NFL-record 22 touchdown passes. However, the 49ers failed to win a postseason game for the third consecutive year, and some fans were fed up. They felt the team's weakness was the 31-year-old Montana. The legendary quarterback also had to worry about talented backup quarterback Steve Young, whom San Francisco had traded for that year.

IN RARE COMPANY

In 1972, the Miami Dolphins set an NFL record by winning all 14 regular season and three postseason games. The NFL later expanded the regular season to 16 games. In 1984, the 49ers went 15–1 before winning three playoff games. That made them the first team with 18 wins in a season. Forty years later, only two other teams had matched that feat.

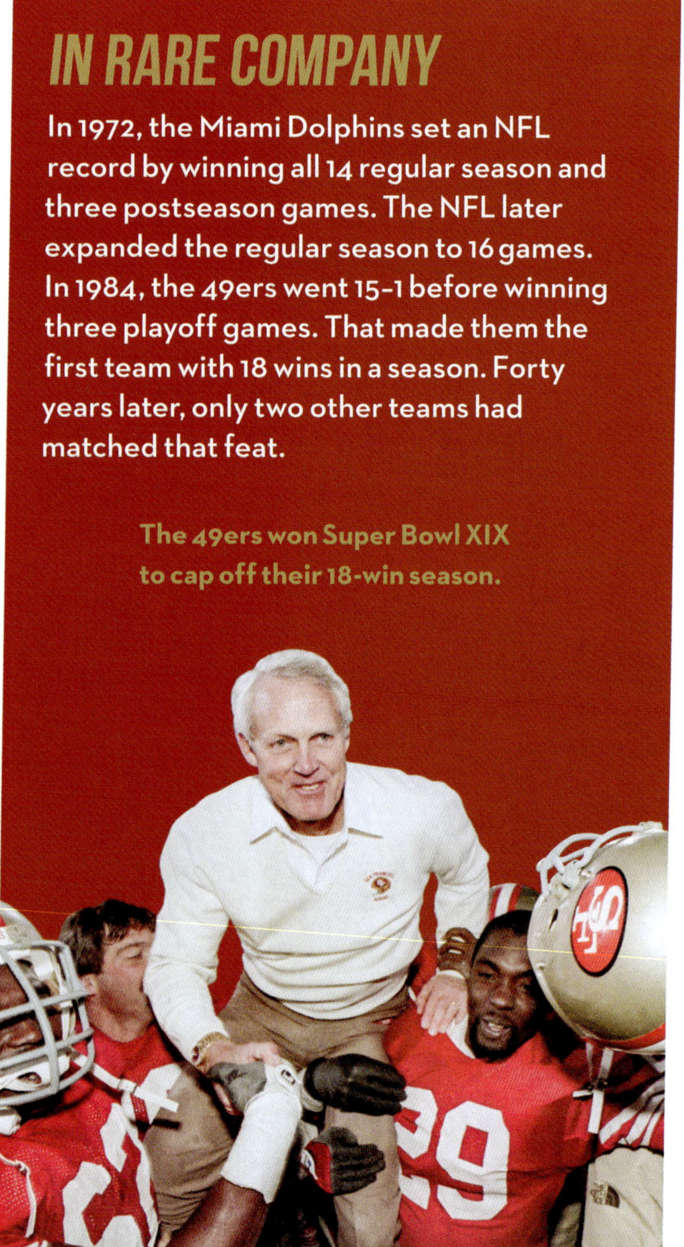

The 49ers won Super Bowl XIX to cap off their 18-win season.

Walsh stuck with Montana in 1988, although Young did play some games that year. The team struggled to a 6–5 start. After Lott called a team meeting to get the 49ers back on the same page, they won four of their last five regular-season games. Montana was healthy and playing well, and the 49ers rolled into the playoffs.

Walsh had hinted at retiring before the season, and he desperately wanted to go out on top. Luckily, the 49ers

Receiver Jerry Rice (80) led the NFL in receiving yards six times during his career.

found their stride in the playoffs, routing both the Bears and the Minnesota Vikings to get back to the Super Bowl. Once again, San Francisco faced the Bengals for the title.

MAKE IT THREE

Super Bowl XXIII was a tight, offensive struggle for the 49ers through three quarters. San Francisco didn't find the end zone until Montana connected with Rice on a 14-yard touchdown pass early in the fourth quarter. The score tied the game at 13–13.

The Bengals responded with a field goal to retake the lead with just over three minutes remaining. After the 49ers were backed up

Defensive end Charles Haley, *in red*, recorded two sacks in Super Bowl XXIII in January 1989.

to their own 8-yard line on the kickoff, several players were nervous in the huddle. Tackle Harris Barton remembered Montana pointing out a famous comedian sitting in the stands.

Moments such as that were why Montana was known as "Joe Cool." And over the next 11 plays, he methodically moved San Francisco down the field. With 34 seconds left, the 49ers faced second-and-goal at the Cincinnati 10-yard line. Many people expected Montana to look for Rice, who was on his way to a record-setting game with 11 catches for 215 yards. Instead, the quarterback fired a pass to his other top receiver, John Taylor. Taylor scored the winning touchdown to secure the 49ers a 20–16 victory and their third Super Bowl title.

In the locker room after the game, an emotional Walsh announced his retirement to his players. It marked the end of one of the most successful coaching eras in league history. In a decade, Walsh had taken the 49ers from being one of the worst teams in the NFL to one of the most dominant teams.

Receiver John Taylor, *right*, prepares to catch the game-winning touchdown to help the 49ers claim their third Super Bowl title.

Linebacker Keena Turner was a key defensive player on all four of the 49ers' championship teams during the 1980s.

CHAPTER 4

RECORD SETTERS

ENTERING THE 1989 NFL SEASON, ONLY THREE TEAMS HAD WON back-to-back Super Bowls, and no team had done it in a decade. The 49ers had a chance to become the fourth, but they would have to do so with a new head coach. George Seifert, who had been Bill Walsh's defensive coordinator since 1983, took over the job.

Seifert was known to be very superstitious. Among his habits was that he refused to ever step on the 49ers logo on the field. "I didn't want to walk on it just out of respect for it and my passion for the San Francisco 49ers," he said.

On the field, not much changed for the 49ers. During the 1989 season, Joe Montana was as good as ever. The quarterback set an NFL record with a passer rating of 112.4. With 26 touchdowns and only eight interceptions, he won his first

Joe Montana runs the ball during Super Bowl XXIV in January 1990.

league MVP Award. Jerry Rice also had a great year, leading the NFL with 1,483 receiving yards and 17 touchdown catches. The 49ers went 14–2, losing both games by a combined five points. The team didn't slow down in the playoffs. San Francisco beat the Minnesota Vikings, who had the top-ranked defense, in the divisional round 41–13. A week later, the 49ers defeated the Los Angeles Rams 30–3 to make it to their second straight Super Bowl.

MONTANA TO RICE

In the week leading up to the Super Bowl XXIV matchup between the 49ers and Denver Broncos, Seifert realized he forgot his lucky sweater. He had worn it for every game during his first season as

Jerry Rice celebrates his early touchdown in Super Bowl XXIV.

head coach. The sweater was sent to Seifert, and he believed he avoided disaster when it arrived the day before the game.

On the field in New Orleans, Montana and Rice didn't need any luck. On the 10th play of San Francisco's opening drive, Montana dropped back from the Denver 20 and fired a pass to Rice at around the 7-yard line. The receiver bounced off a hit, then raced into the end zone holding the ball above his head in celebration.

That was the start of a historic performance for the pair. Montana threw a Super Bowl-record five touchdown passes. Rice caught three of them to set another record. San Francisco dominated the Broncos 55–10 in the largest blowout in Super Bowl history.

CHANGING OF THE GUARD

The 49ers returned in 1990 primed to win their third straight title. Montana won the league MVP Award again. Rice became the

Montana (16) tries to scramble away from New York Giants defenders in the NFC title game on January 20, 1991.

first player in modern NFL history to lead the league in catches, receiving yards, and receiving touchdowns in one season.

The team reached the NFC title game and faced the New York Giants. In a brutal, hard-hitting contest, neither offense could get much going. The 49ers led 13–9 late in the fourth quarter when Montana was knocked from the game by a blindside hit. After the Giants kicked another field goal, Steve Young came on to try to get the 49ers to the Super Bowl again. But a fumble by running back Roger Craig gave the ball back to the Giants, who ended San Francisco's run on a last-second field goal to win 15–13.

The loss began a period of change for the 49ers. Craig left in the offseason, as did Ronnie Lott. Montana then missed the 1991 season and most of 1992 season due to injuries, giving Young the starting position. After the younger quarterback earned the league's MVP Award in 1992, the 49ers decided to move on from Montana for good. Although team owner Eddie DeBartolo didn't want to, he allowed the team to trade Montana to the Kansas City Chiefs in 1993.

Young had the job, but he needed to prove himself in the playoffs. The 49ers had reached the NFC title game in each of his first two seasons as the full-time starter. However, they fell both times to the Dallas Cowboys.

As Young entered the 1994 season, the quarterback still hadn't escaped being compared to Montana. The only way he could get out of the legend's shadow was to win a Super Bowl title. Young won the regular-season MVP once again after completing more than 70 percent of his passes and throwing a league-leading 35 touchdowns. And 32-year-old Rice was still the NFL's best receiver. The 49ers became just the fourth team in league history to top 500 points in a season. The defense was anchored by cornerback Deion Sanders, who was so dominant that opposing quarterbacks rarely threw the ball near him.

San Francisco finished the 1994 season 13–3 to land a spot

Cornerback Deion Sanders was named the NFL Defensive Player of the Year during his one season with the 49ers in 1994.

in the playoffs. After routing the Chicago Bears in the divisional round, the 49ers once again faced the Cowboys in the NFC title game. The two fierce rivals were so dominant that the game was billed as "the Real Super Bowl." Behind two touchdown passes and one rushing score from Young in front of their home crowd in Candlestick Park, the 49ers outlasted Dallas 38–28.

Quarterback Steve Young, *right*, and Rice celebrate after scoring a touchdown in Super Bowl XXIX in January 1995.

The 49ers were considered huge favorites against the San Diego Chargers in Super Bowl XXIX. And just as Montana and Rice had done five years earlier, Young and Rice got the team off to a hot start. On the third play of the game, Young heaved a pass down the middle toward the star receiver. Rice beat two defenders to the catch and raced to the end zone for a 44-yard score.

The play set the tone for another Super Bowl romp by the 49ers. Young topped Montana's Super Bowl–touchdown record by tossing six scores, with Rice catching three of them. San Francisco won the game 49–26 to become the first team to win five Super Bowl titles. Young was named the game's MVP for his record-setting performance. But more importantly, he had finally freed himself from Montana's shadow and erased any doubts that he couldn't win the big game.

ONE MORE "CATCH"

By Super Bowl XXIX, Young was already 33 years old. But as the 1990s wore on, he seemed ageless. Young led the NFL in completion percentage that year, and he continued to do so his next three seasons. The 49ers won the NFC West twice but failed

Tackle Dana Stubblefield (94) was named the NFL Defensive Rookie of the Year in 1993.

to advance past the divisional round in the playoffs in 1995 and 1996. After the 1996 season, Seifert resigned. Steve Mariucci, who was a former college head coach, took over and led the team to a 13–3 record in 1997. However, San Francisco lost 23–10 in the NFC Championship Game to the Green Bay Packers.

By 1998, many of the 49ers' top stars were gone. Young and Rice remained, but the team was also trying to get many of the younger players more experience. One of the best was third-year receiver Terrell Owens, who led the team with 14 touchdown catches that year. At 6 feet, 3 inches and 224 pounds, Owens was tough for defenders to handle. He appeared primed to take over for Rice as San Francisco's next receiving star.

RICE'S NUMBERS

Jerry Rice left the 49ers after the 2000 season as one of the greatest receivers in NFL history. From 1986 to 1996, Rice had 1,000 or more receiving yards each season. He recorded double-digit touchdowns in all but two of those years. Rice set numerous NFL records and holds every major 49er receiving record, including receptions, receiving yards, and receiving touchdowns.

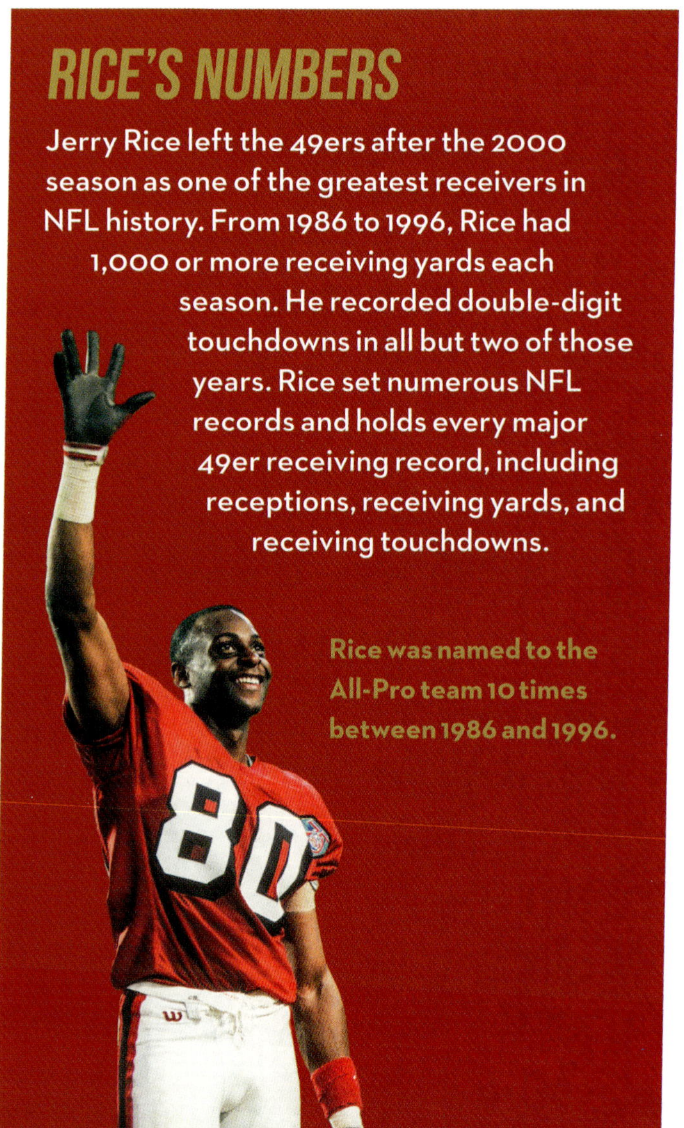

Rice was named to the All-Pro team 10 times between 1986 and 1996.

Young led the NFL in touchdown passes as the team finished the 1998 season 12–4. Although the 49ers didn't win the NFC West, they had a good enough record to host the Packers in the wild-card round. The teams put on a thrilling contest, with the lead changing hands six times during the game. With two minutes to go, Green Bay went ahead 27–23 on a 15-yard touchdown pass. Young and the 49ers needed to respond fast.

The veteran quarterback slowly guided San Francisco down the field by mixing his passes to several receivers. The one player Young struggled to connect with, though, was Owens. The 25-year-old had caught only two passes and had dropped several more chances during the game.

With eight seconds left, San Francisco faced third down at the Green Bay 25. The 49ers didn't have any timeouts and knew they had to go for the end zone. Young tripped as he dropped back but recovered in time to rifle a pass down the middle of the field. Owens caught the ball at the goal line, then held on for a touchdown as he was hit by Packers defenders. The miracle grab won the game for San Francisco. Hearkening back to Dwight Clark's famous play in the NFC title game against the Cowboys, Owens's grab was dubbed "the Catch II." San Francisco lost in the divisional round a week later, but the play lived on as one of the most memorable finishes in 49ers history.

Receiver Terrell Owens, *center*, catches the game-winning touchdown in the playoff game between the 49ers and the Green Bay Packers in January 1999.

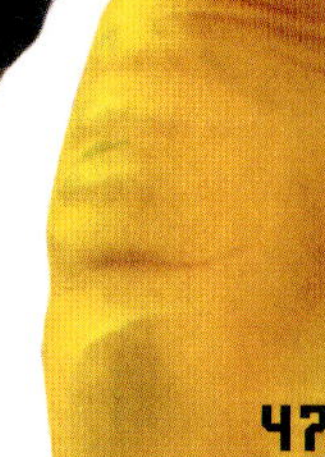

Quarterback Jeff Garcia (5) and the 49ers huddle during a game against the St. Louis Rams in 2001.

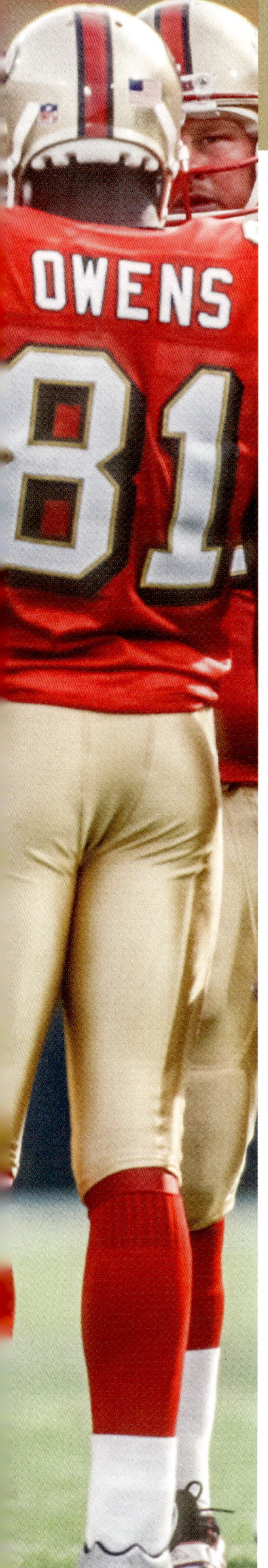

CHAPTER 5

GOLDEN AGAIN

In Week 3 of the 1999 season, Steve Young dropped back to pass against the Arizona Cardinals. As Young released the ball, two Cardinals defenders slammed into the 49ers' signal-caller, and he suffered a concussion. It was the seventh concussion of his career. Young never played again.

The injury signaled the end of the 49ers' two decades of success between 1980 and 2000. Even bringing Bill Walsh back to a front office position in 1999 failed to get the team back on track. Between 1999 and 2010, the 49ers reached the playoffs just twice. Their only postseason win in that span came after the 2002 regular season, although it was a memorable one. The team erased a 24-point second-half deficit to beat the New York Giants 39–38.

Running back Frank Gore (21) became the 49ers' all-time leading rusher in 2011.

Despite the team's struggles in the standings, 49ers fans were treated to several star performances. Terrell Owens had three All-Pro seasons before being traded after the 2003 season. Two years later, Frank Gore debuted, and the sturdy running back stayed with the 49ers for 10 seasons. He reached 1,000 yards in eight of them and left the team with 11,073 rushing yards and 75 total touchdowns. Gore shared the spotlight for most of those years with tough linebacker Patrick Willis. Willis anchored the defense from 2007 through 2014, earning five All-Pro selections before retiring due to injuries at 29.

HARBAUGH BALL

In 2011, San Francisco went back to the college ranks to find its new head coach. The 49ers hired Jim Harbaugh, a former NFL quarterback who, like Walsh, had been coaching at Stanford. The energetic Harbaugh loved tough, physical football. He also earned the trust of his players by treating them well. General manager Trent Baalke said of Harbaugh, "What we have to do is bring back the culture of winning. He's a guy who can lead the 49ers franchise back to where it rightfully belongs."

"WHAT WE HAVE TO DO IS BRING BACK THE CULTURE OF WINNING. [HARBAUGH IS] A GUY WHO CAN LEAD THE 49ERS FRANCHISE BACK TO WHERE IT RIGHTFULLY BELONGS."

—TRENT BAALKE

Harbaugh quickly turned San Francisco around. With former first-round draft pick Alex Smith leading the offense at quarterback, the 49ers finished 13–3 and won the NFC West for the first time in nine years. In the team's playoff opener, San Francisco dueled the New Orleans Saints. In a wild fourth quarter, the teams combined for 34 points. Smith ended the back-and-forth battle by throwing the winning touchdown to veteran tight end Vernon Davis with nine seconds left. San Francisco won 36–32. A week later in the NFC title game against the Giants, Smith and Davis connected on a 73-yard touchdown pass in the first quarter. But San Francisco ended up falling 20–17 in overtime.

LIGHTS OUT

Smith led the 49ers to another good start in 2012. But in Week 10, he suffered a concussion. Harbaugh turned to second-year backup quarterback Colin Kaepernick, who brought a new dimension to the offense. Kaepernick wasn't as polished in the passing game

Linebacker Patrick Willis was inducted into the Pro Football Hall of Fame in 2024.

as Smith, but he had a strong arm and blazing speed. He led the 49ers to a 5–2 finish in their last seven games. Even when Smith was healthy again, Harbaugh stuck with Kaepernick.

That decision paid off in the divisional round against the Green Bay Packers. Kaepernick threw two touchdown passes and rushed for two more. His second rushing score was a 56-yard burst down the right sideline to break a 24–24 tie. Kaepernick finished the game with 181 rushing yards, a playoff record for a quarterback, to help San Francisco win 45–31.

Quarterback Colin Kaepernick crosses the goal line for one of his two rushing touchdowns in the divisional round of the playoffs in January 2013.

The following week, the 49ers rallied to beat the Atlanta Falcons 28–24 in the NFC title game behind two second-half touchdowns from Gore. With the win, San Francisco earned its first Super Bowl appearance since the 1994 season.

In Super Bowl XLVII, Harbaugh faced his younger brother, John, who was the head coach of the Baltimore Ravens. The family affair, known as "the Harbaugh Bowl," was one-sided into the third quarter, though, as the Ravens raced out to a 28–6 lead.

Suddenly, half the field at the Superdome in New Orleans went dark. The power had failed, and it took more than 30 minutes for stadium workers to get the lights back on. Meanwhile, the teams were stuck on the field. The 49ers' locker room didn't have power, so neither team was allowed to go back underneath the stands.

San Francisco head coach Jim Harbaugh, *right*, chats with his brother, John, the head coach of the Baltimore Ravens, before Super Bowl XLVII on February 3, 2013.

When the lights came back on, the 49ers came alive, scoring 17 points in a row before the Ravens answered with a field goal to make it 31–23. With 9:57 left in the fourth quarter, Kaepernick ran for a 15-yard touchdown to bring the 49ers to within two points. But facing pressure from a blitz on the two-point conversion, Kaepernick misfired on his pass. The 49ers never got any closer, and they lost 34–31.

Throughout the 2013 season, the 49ers battled the division-rival Seattle Seahawks for NFC West dominance. At the end of the year, Seattle won the division. The 49ers won two road playoff games to set up a meeting with the Seahawks in the NFC title game. In an intense, physical battle, San Francisco came up just short. Kaepernick's potential game-tying touchdown pass was intercepted in the end zone in the final seconds of a 23–17 loss.

KAEPERNICK'S PROTEST

Before a preseason game in the 2016 season, quarterback Colin Kaepernick initiated a protest. Kaepernick believed that people of color in the United States were not being treated equally, and he hoped to bring attention to this issue by kneeling for the US national anthem. Many people agreed with Kaepernick. However, others were angered by his refusal to stand for the anthem. Kaepernick believed the protest hurt his career, as he never played in the NFL again after 2016.

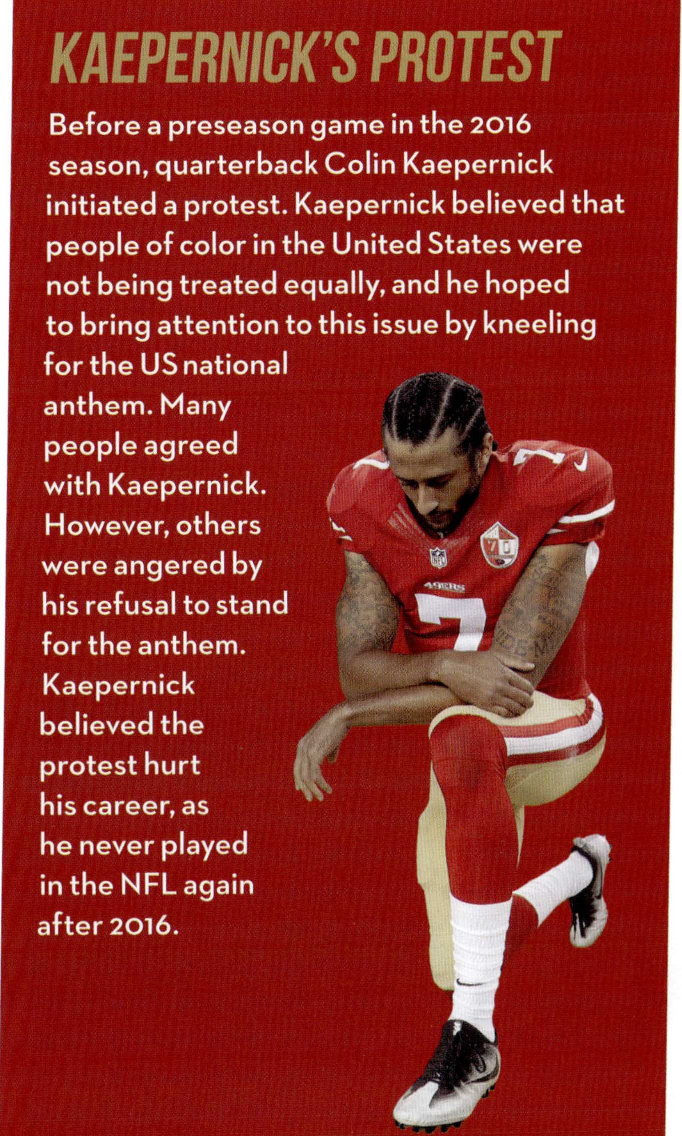

LOOKING FOR MORE

In 2014, the 49ers moved into a new home. Levi's Stadium was built in Santa Clara, which is about 50 miles (80 km) south of San Francisco. But by that year, the 49ers had lost their glow and finished 8–8. After the season, Harbaugh was let go after he disagreed with the front office on how to turn things around.

It took several years for the 49ers to get back on track. After four straight losing seasons, San Francisco began improving under offensive-minded head coach Kyle Shanahan in 2019. The team boasted a top offense led by quarterback Jimmy Garoppolo, rugged tight end George Kittle, and versatile receiver Deebo Samuel. The defense was paced by punishing linebacker Fred Warner and defensive end Nick Bosa, who was named the NFL's Defensive Rookie of the Year.

The 49ers finished 13–3, then raced back to the Super Bowl to take on the Kansas City Chiefs. Midway through the fourth quarter, San Francisco led 20–10. But Kansas City's star quarterback Patrick Mahomes led a comeback, and the 49ers crumbled late and lost 31–20.

Despite the defeat, San Francisco looked set up for a long run at the top of the NFC. Injuries to Bosa, Garoppolo, and Kittle knocked the team off course in 2020. The trio returned to lead the 49ers to the NFC title game a year later, but the team suffered another fourth-quarter meltdown against the Los Angeles Rams. Leading 17–7 entering the quarter, San Francisco ended up losing 20–17.

After injuries to both Garoppolo and top draft pick Trey Lance during the 2021 season, the team turned to unknown rookie quarterback Brock Purdy. Few people expected Purdy to succeed, but he teamed up with Samuel and Kittle, along with speedy

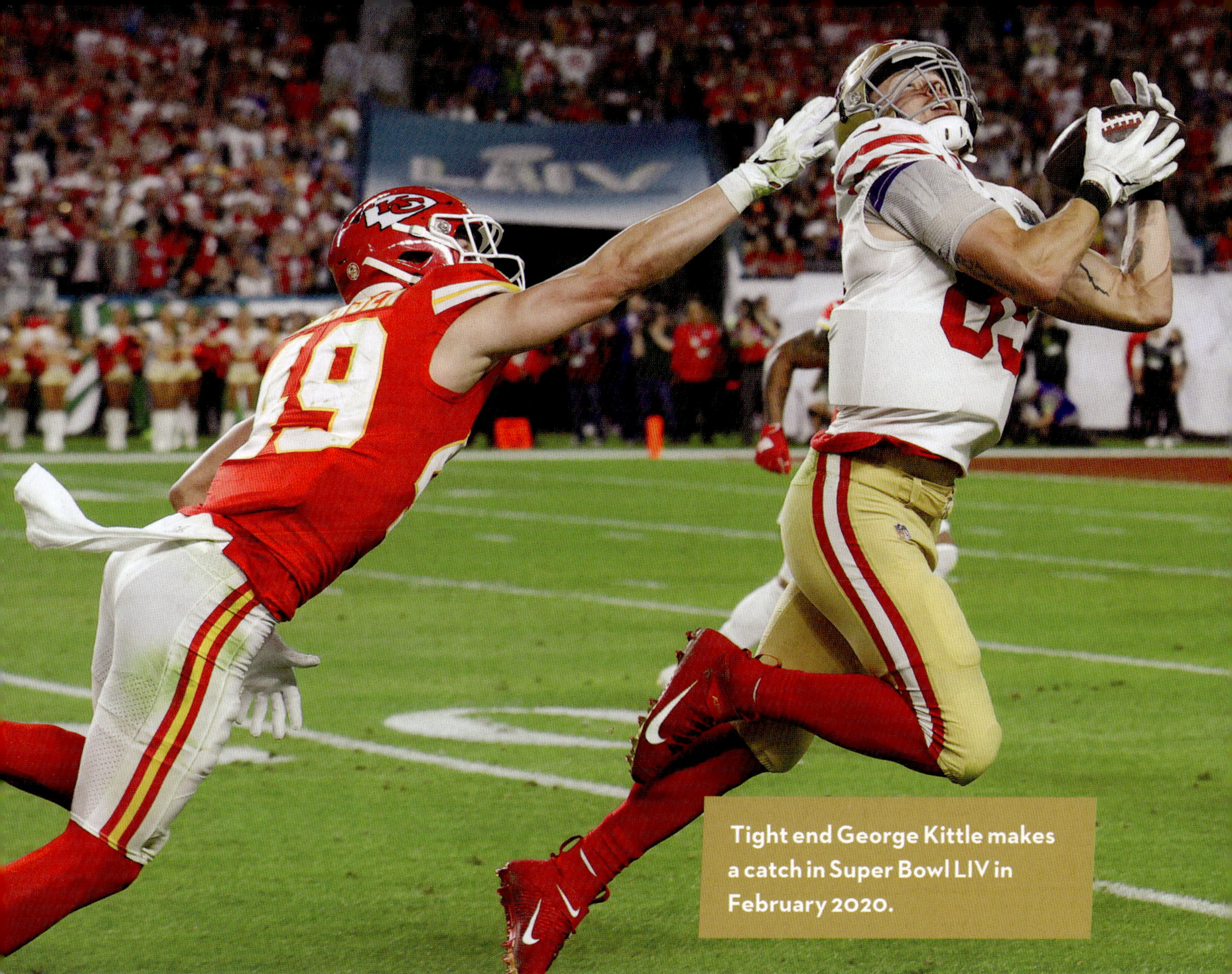

Tight end George Kittle makes a catch in Super Bowl LIV in February 2020.

receiver Brandon Aiyuk and dual-threat runner Christian McCaffrey. Purdy threw 11 touchdown passes in five starts, then led the 49ers to a pair of playoff wins to reach the NFC title game. But after an arm injury forced Purdy out of the game, San Francisco lost 31–7 to the Philadelphia Eagles.

In 2023, the 49ers finally stayed healthy, and Purdy proved his rookie year was no fluke. He threw 31 touchdown passes during the 2023 season. McCaffrey was named the Offensive Player of the Year after leading the league in rushing with 1,459 yards while also scoring 21 total touchdowns.

49ERS TROPHY CASE

SUPER BOWL CHAMPIONSHIPS: 5

Super Bowl XVI – January 24, 1982
Super Bowl XIX – January 20, 1985
Super Bowl XXIII – January 22, 1989
Super Bowl XXIV – January 28, 1990
Super Bowl XXIX – January 29, 1995

CONFERENCE CHAMPIONSHIPS: 8

1981, 1984, 1988, 1989, 1994, 2012, 2019, 2023

DIVISION TITLES: 22

NFC West: 1970, 1971, 1972, 1981, 1983, 1984, 1986, 1987, 1988, 1989, 1990, 1992, 1993, 1994, 1995, 1997, 2002, 2011, 2012, 2019, 2022, 2023

All stats are through the 2024 season.

After a thrilling comeback win against the Detroit Lions in the NFC title game, the 49ers went back to the Super Bowl. They once again matched up with the Chiefs. Kansas City was the defending champion, but the 49ers jumped out to a 10–3 lead in the first half of Super Bowl LVIII. However, the 49ers couldn't hold it. Despite having a 19–16 edge with less than two minutes to play, the 49ers gave up a game-tying field goal before losing 25–22 in overtime.

The 49ers entered 2024 with hopes of winning the Super Bowl. But injuries to multiple key stars derailed their season, leading to a disappointing 6–11 record. Despite the struggles, fans hoped the team's talented group of players could bounce back and add another title to the franchise's collection.

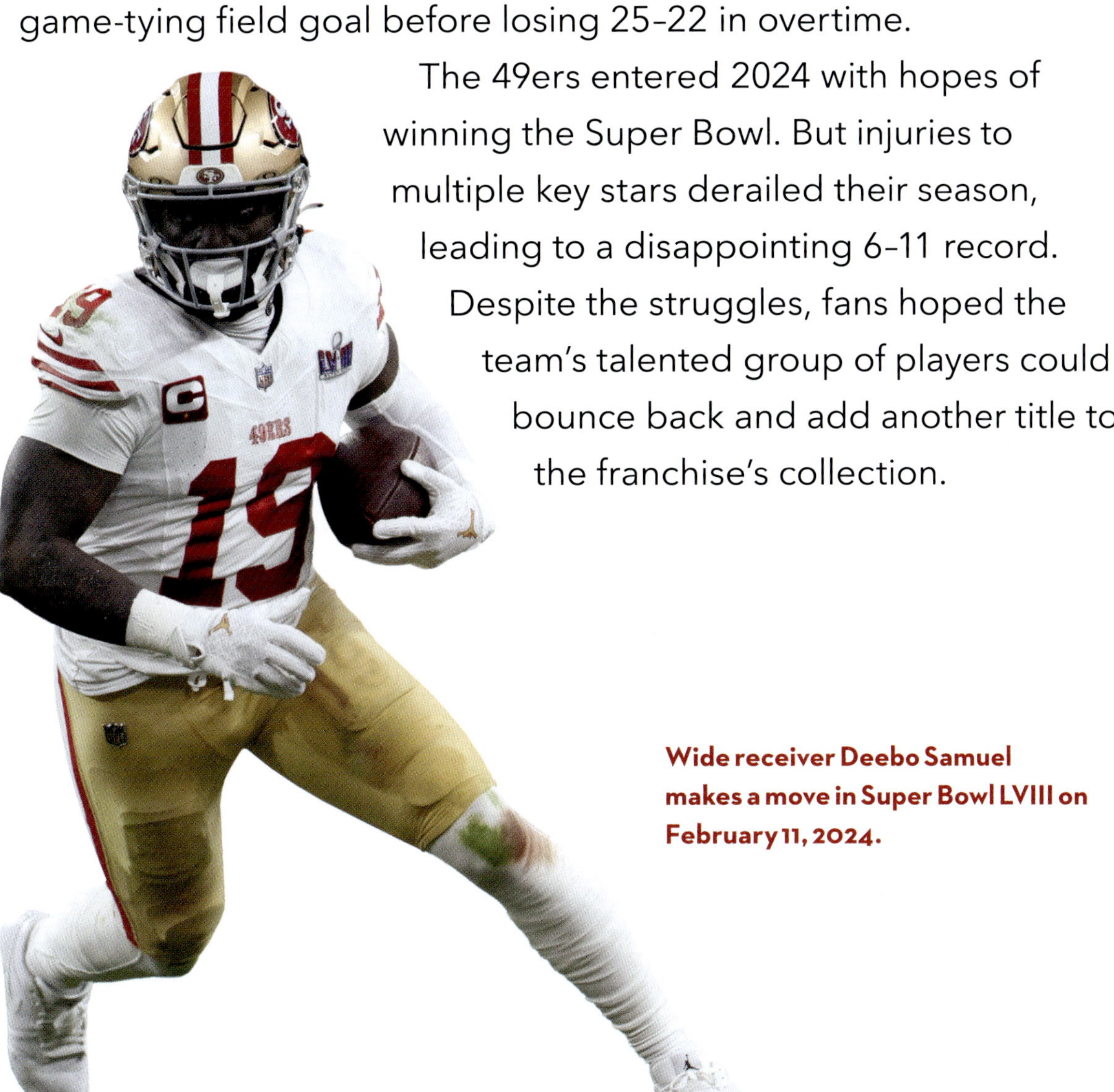

Wide receiver Deebo Samuel makes a move in Super Bowl LVIII on February 11, 2024.

TIMELINE

The San Francisco 49ers begin play in the AAFC.
1946

1949
The 49ers play in their first AAFC Championship Game but lose to the Cleveland Browns.

After the AAFC folds, the 49ers join the NFL.
1950

1957
The 49ers make their first NFL playoff appearance but lose to the Detroit Lions.

San Francisco hires head coach Bill Walsh and selects quarterback Joe Montana in the draft.
1979

1982
Montana leads the 49ers to win their first Super Bowl title on January 24.

The 49ers set a franchise record with 18 wins after winning Super Bowl XIX on January 20.
1985

1990
After an MVP season from Montana, the 49ers win their second straight Super Bowl title on January 28.

In Super Bowl XXIX on January 29, quarterback Steve Young sets an NFL record with six touchdown passes to help the 49ers beat the San Diego Chargers.
1995

2013
Head coach Jim Harbaugh leads the 49ers back to the Super Bowl on February 3, but they lose to the Baltimore Ravens.

Under coach Kyle Shanahan, San Francisco loses to the Kansas City Chiefs in Super Bowl LIV on February 2.
2020

2024
The 49ers secure a comeback victory against the Lions in the NFC title game on January 28.

GLOSSARY

amateur—a person who plays a sport without getting paid.

backfield—the set of players, including quarterback and running backs, who line up behind the offensive line.

blitz—when a linebacker or defensive back attacks the line of scrimmage to stop a run or sack the quarterback.

comeback—a big rally after falling behind.

concussion—a brain injury caused by a blow to the head or a violent shaking of the head and body.

coordinator—an assistant coach who is in charge of the offense, defense, or special teams.

draft—a system that allows teams to acquire new players coming into the league.

favorite—the person or team that is expected to win.

franchise—an entire sports organization.

general manager—an executive who runs a team and is responsible for finding and signing players.

interception—a pass that is caught by a defensive player.

pick six—an interception returned for a touchdown.

Pro Bowl—a postseason competition that the NFL's all-stars are invited to compete in.

professional—a person who gets paid to perform.

rival—an opponent with whom a player or team has a fierce and ongoing competition.

rookie—a professional athlete in his or her first year of competition.

superstitious—a belief or practice that involves magic or luck.

turnover—loss of the ball to the other team through an interception or fumble.

two-point conversion—an option for teams that have scored a touchdown to try a running or passing play from the 2-yard line for two points, instead of kicking for one point.

upset—an unexpected victory by a supposedly weaker team or player.

veteran—someone who has played for many years.

ONLINE RESOURCES

To learn more about the San Francisco 49ers, please visit **abdobooklinks.com** or scan this QR code. These links are routinely monitored and updated to provide the most current information available.

INDEX